Never Take a Pig to Lunch

And Other Poems About The Fun Of Eating

Never Take a Pig to Lunch

And Other Poems About The Fun Of Eating

Selected and Illustrated by

Nadine Bernard Westcott

ORCHARD BOOKS
New York

LOOK OUT, STOMACH, HERE IT COMES!

Poems about eating silly things

Contents

WE ALL SCREAM FOR ICE CREAM
Poems about eating foods we like

NEVER EAT MORE THAN YOU CAN LIFT

Poems about Eating too much

MY MOTHER SAYS I'M SICKENING
Poems about manners at the table

To the friends and family who have sat at my table.—N.B.W.

THROUGH the teeth
And past the gums—
Look out, stomach,
Here it comes!
ANONYMOUS

EELS

Poems about
eating silly things

A FISHERMAN LIVING IN DEAL

A fisherman living in Deal,
When asked what he liked for a meal,
Said, "All kinds of fish,
But my favorite dish
Is a properly stuffed jellied eel."

CHARLES CONNELL

THE CANTANKEROUS 'GATOR

There was a cantankerous 'gator
For whom 'twas no pleasure to cater.
  If he happened to find
  No dish to his mind,
He would like as not swallow the waiter.

OLIVER HERFORD

10

A gourmet challenged me to eat
A tiny bit of rattlesnake meat,
Remarking, "Don't look horror-stricken,
You'll find it tastes a lot like chicken."
It did.
Now chicken I cannot eat
Because it tastes like rattlesnake meat.

OGDEN NASH

EELS

Eileen Carroll
Had a barrel
Filled with writhing eels
And just for fun
She swallowed one:
Now she knows how it feels.

SPIKE MILLIGAN

The Eel

I don't mind eels
Except as meals.
And the way they feels.

OGDEN NASH

11

8−1=7   3+2=5   1+1=2   9−3=6

$$\begin{array}{r} 2 \\ +2 \\ \hline 4 \end{array}$$

$$\begin{array}{r} 3 \\ +2 \\ \hline 5 \end{array}$$

$$\begin{array}{r} 6 \\ -2 \\ \hline 4 \end{array}$$

$$\begin{array}{r} 2 \\ -1 \\ \hline 1 \end{array}$$

$$\begin{array}{r} 5 \\ +3 \\ \hline 8 \end{array}$$

$$\begin{array}{r} 4 \\ +3 \\ \hline 7 \end{array}$$

$$\begin{array}{r} 2 \\ +1 \\ \hline 3 \end{array}$$

$$\begin{array}{r} 9 \\ +4 \\ \hline 8 \end{array}$$

$$\begin{array}{r} 2 \\ +5 \\ \hline 7 \end{array}$$

$$\begin{array}{r} 3 \\ -2 \\ \hline 1 \end{array}$$

$$\begin{array}{r} 5 \\ +1 \\ \hline 6 \end{array}$$

$$\begin{array}{r} 4 \\ +2 \\ \hline 6 \end{array}$$

$$\begin{array}{r} 2 \\ +6 \\ \hline 8 \end{array}$$

$$\begin{array}{r} 3 \\ -2 \\ \hline \end{array}$$

Could anything be drearier
Than the food in the school cafeteria?

FLORENCE PARRY HEIDE AND ROXANNE HEIDE PIERCE

School Lunch

Each time I bring it
I wish I had bought it
But each time I buy it
I wish I had brought it.

MARY ANN HOBERMAN

7−4=3   9+1=10   5+4=9

BALONEY!

Jim opened his lunchbox
and peered inside.
"I'm hungry, I'm starving,
I'm famished," he sighed.
"Oh, baloney," he said,
"it's baloney again!
I'd like something different,
at least now and then.
Baloney with mustard,
baloney with cheese,
baloney with mayo,
baloney—oh, please.
I've had it all week
and the week before that
and the week before *that*
and the week before THAT.
I've had it for lunch
every day of the year.
Baloney, if only
you'd just disappear."
"Why not make your own sandwich?"
I suggested to him.
"What a brilliant idea—
you're a genius," said Jim.
"I do make my own,"
he admitted with pride,
"but baloney's the only one I've ever tried!"

FLORENCE PARRY HEIDE

13

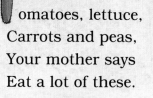

Tomatoes, lettuce,
Carrots and peas,
Your mother says
Eat a lot of these.

Celery, raw,
Develops the jaw,
But celery, stewed,
Is more quietly chewed.

OGDEN NASH

The Parsnip

The parsnip, children, I repeat
Is simply an anemic beet.
Some people call the parsnip edible;
Myself, I find this claim incredible.

OGDEN NASH

14

PECULIAR

I once knew a boy who was odd as could be:
He liked to eat cauliflower and broccoli
And spinach and turnips and rhubarb pies
And he didn't like hamburgers or French fries.

EVE MERRIAM

Arbuckle Jones

Arbuckle Jones
When flustered
Eats custard
With mustard.

I'm disgustard.

PETER WESLEY-SMITH

A (Pretty) Good Recipe for Pie

Take a pound of chicken feathers,
Put 'em in a crust.
Stomp 'em on the driveway,
Sprinkle 'em with rust.

Scrunch up the mixture
in a lumpy little ball.
Add a pound of rubber bands.
Fling it at the wall.

Wrap it all up
in an old monkey skin.
Kick it out the window.
Kick it back in.

1 lb. Rubber Bands

Rust

Open up the monkey skin.
Add some plasticine.
If your mother catches you
tell her to mind-her-own-business-or-she'll-
   have-to-go-to-her-room-without-her-
   supper-and-won't-be-able-to-watch-
   tv-for-a-week-or-stay-up-late-or-
   have-her-friends-over-and-furthermore-
   that-she-won't-get-any-allowance-
   young-lady-and-that-you're-not-
   kidding-this-time-either-because-
   you're-entirely-fed-up-THANK-you.

Bake it in the bottom drawer
at 35 degrees.
Cool it in the bathtub
and serve with cheddar cheese.

(serves six)

CHARLES WILKINS

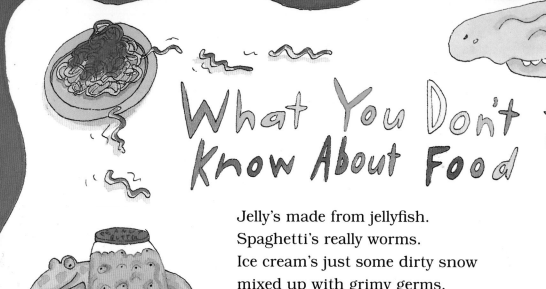

What You Don't Know About Food

Jelly's made from jellyfish.
Spaghetti's really worms.
Ice cream's just some dirty snow
mixed up with grimy germs.
Bread is made of glue and paste.
So are cakes and pies.
Peanut butter's filled with stuff
like squashed-up lizard eyes.
And as you eat potato chips,
remember all the while—
they're slices of the dried-up brain
of some old crocodile.

FLORENCE PARRY HEIDE

O Sliver
of Liver

O sliver of liver,
Get lost! Go away!
You tremble and quiver
O sliver of liver—
You set me a-shiver
And spoil my day—
O sliver of liver,
Get lost! Go away!

MYRA COHN LIVINGSTON

Swallow a Slug
By its tail or its snout
Feel it slide down
Feel it climb out

DAVID GREENBERG

THE WORM

When the earth is turned in spring
The worms are fat as anything.

And birds come flying all around
To eat the worms right off the ground.

They like worms just as much as I
Like bread and milk and apple pie.

And once, when I was very young,
I put a worm right on my tongue.

I didn't like the taste a bit,
And so I didn't swallow it.

But oh, it makes my Mother squirm
Because she *thinks* I ate that worm!

RALPH BERGENGREN

19

EATING WITH AN ALLIGATOR ISN'T QUITE THE THING!

I was reading in a restaurant,
   enjoying sunshine spring,
When a 'gator in a top hat smiled a very
   toothy grin.
He headed for my table, and he sat down
   by my side,
He said he felt quite hungry, and his huge
   jaws opened wide.

So I handed him a menu, which he
   chewed up into shreds,
Then proceeded very quickly, to eat the
   table spreads!
I tried to look quite calm and cool,
   And cover up my fright,
Suppose he saw me as a meal—
   For him a tempting sight!

He chomped up all the table legs—
   The silver service too,
Then looked at me and whispered,
   "I won't partake of you—
For although you look quite tasty,
   In your padded suit and tie,
Your face is much too pasty
   For a 'gator such as I!!"

ANGELA SIDEY

SPAGHETTI! SPAGHETTI!

Spaghetti! spaghetti!
you're wonderful stuff,
I love you, spaghetti,
I can't get enough.
You're covered with sauce
and you're sprinkled with cheese,
spaghetti! spaghetti!
oh, give me some more please.

Spaghetti! spaghetti!
piled high in a mound,
you wiggle, you wriggle,
you squiggle around.
There's slurpy spaghetti
all over my plate,
spaghetti! spaghetti!
I think you are great.

Spaghetti! spaghetti!
I love you a lot,
you're slishy, you're sloshy,
delicious and hot.
I gobble you down
oh, I can't get enough,
spaghetti! spaghetti!
you're wonderful stuff.

JACK PRELUTSKY

LASAGNA

Wouldn't you love
To have lasagna
Any old time
The mood was on ya?

X. J. KENNEDY

HOW DO YOU MAKE A PIZZA GROW?

How do you make a pizza grow?

You pound and you pull and you stretch the dough
And throw in tomatoes and oregano.

Pizza platter for twenty-two,
Pour on the oil and soak it through.

Pizza slices for forty-four,
Chop up onions, make some more.

Pizza pie for sixty-six
With mozzarella cheese that melts and sticks.

Pizza pizza for ninety-nine
With pepperoni sausage ground-up fine.

Pizza pizza stretch the dough,
Pizza pizza make it grow.

EVE MERRIAM

Oodles of Noodles

I love noodles. Give me oodles.
Make a mound up to the sun.
Noodles are my favorite foodles.
I eat noodles by the ton.

LUCIA AND JAMES L. HYMES, JR.

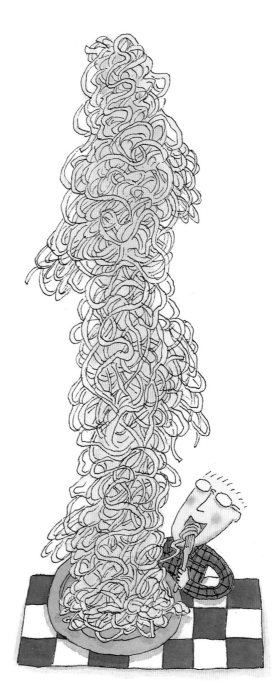

IT'S HOT!

Tonight
I have a bite
of Uncle Willie's chili . . .

O wow!
it's hot!
and how!

my eyes start to sting
my ears start to ring
          it's hot!

I gasp and I wheeze
I cough and I sneeze
          it's hot!

my stomach's in a knot
and every single spot
          is hot!

it tickles my nose
it burns down to my toes
and up again
and makes my hair
stand on end
          it's hot!

Uncle Willie, Uncle Willie,
may I please have some more
of this delicious chili?

FLORENCE PARRY HEIDE

Peanut Butter and Jelly

First you take the dough and knead it,
  knead it.
Peanut butter, peanut butter, jelly, jelly.
Pop it in the oven and bake it, bake it.
Peanut butter, peanut butter, jelly, jelly.
Then you take a knife and slice it, slice it.
Peanut butter, peanut butter, jelly, jelly.
Then you take the peanuts and crack them,
  crack them.
Peanut butter, peanut butter, jelly, jelly.
Put them on the floor and mash them,
  mash them.
Peanut butter, peanut butter, jelly, jelly.
Then you take a knife and spread it, spread it.
Peanut butter, peanut butter, jelly, jelly.
Next you take some grapes and squash them,
  squash them.
Peanut butter, peanut butter, jelly, jelly.
Glop it on the bread and smear it, smear it.
Peanut butter, peanut butter, jelly, jelly.
Then you take the sandwich and eat it, eat it.
Peanut butter, peanut butter, jelly, jelly.

ANONYMOUS

Yellow butter purple jelly red jam black bread

Spread it thick
Say it quick

Yellow butter purple jelly red jam black bread

Spread it thicker
Say it quicker

Yellow butter purple jelly red jam black bread

Now repeat it
While you eat it

Yellow butter purple jelly red jam black bread

Don't talk
With your mouth full!

MARY ANN HOBERMAN

PURPLE JELLY ... RED JAM ... BLACK BREAD

Successful Pancakes

There's a trick to making pancakes
that everyone should know.
The trick is this, to flatten them
as flat as they will go.

Hit 'em with a dictionary.
Hit 'em with a ski.
Hit 'em with an elephant.
Hit 'em with a tree.

. . . till they're

Flatter than a splisher,
Flatter than a splat,
Flatter than a pancake,
Flat, flat, FLAT.

Throw 'em in the frying pan.
Flip 'em on their backs.
Cook 'em till you think they're done
and throw 'em down the hatch.

CHARLES WILKINS

PICNICS

Sunshine and weiners and pickles and ham,
  Not enough salt for the eggs,
Marshmallows cooked on the end of a stick,
  Ants crawling over our legs.

Candy and cookies and peanuts and cake,
  Finding the frosting has run,
All of us knowing we've eaten too much—
  Picnics are certainly fun!

MARCHETTE CHUTE

The Picnic

We brought a rug for sitting on,
Our lunch was in a box.
The sand was warm. We didn't wear
Hats or Shoes or Socks.

Waves came curling up the beach.
We waded. It was fun.
Our sandwiches were different kinds.
I dropped my jelly one.

DOROTHY ALDIS

SNOW-CONE

Snow-cone nice
Snow-cone sweet
Snow-cone is crush ice
and good for the heat.

When sun really hot
and I thirsty a lot,
Me alone,
Yes me alone,
could eat ten snow-cone.

If you think is lie I tell
wait till you hear the snow-cone bell,
wait till you hear the snow-cone bell.

JOHN AGARD

FUDGE!

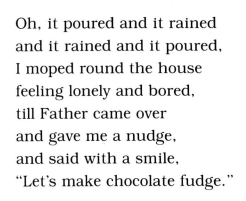

Oh, it poured and it rained
and it rained and it poured,
I moped round the house
feeling lonely and bored,
till Father came over
and gave me a nudge,
and said with a smile,
"Let's make chocolate fudge."

Then he gave me a bowl
that we filled to the brim,
it was fun making fudge
in the kitchen with him.
I stirred and I stirred,
but I wasn't too neat,
I got fudge on my hands,
I got fudge on my feet,
I got fudge on my shirt,
I got fudge in my hair,
I got fudge on the table
and fudge on the chair,
I got fudge in my nose,
I got fudge in my ears,
I was covered all over
with chocolate smears.

When the cooking was done,
Father wiped off my face,
and he frowned as he said,
"What a mess in this place!"
He was not really mad
and did not hold a grudge,
and we both ate a mountain
of chocolate fudge.

JACK PRELUTSKY

"I want my breakfast,"
   The giant said,
"The minute that I wake up
   In my giant bed.

"Tell the kitchen,"
   The giant said,
"I'm giantly hungry,
   And I better get fed.

"I don't want oatmeal
   Or eggs with toast.
I want what I want
   And I want it the most.

"One hundred pancakes
   And not one less,
And enough maple syrup
   To make a giant mess."

EVE MERRIAM

34

SAID A LONG CROCODILE

Said a very l—o—n—g crocodile,
"My length is a terrible trial!
I know I should diet
But each time I try it
I'm hungry for more than a mile!"

LILIAN MOORE

The Vulture

The vulture eats between his meals,
    And that's the reason why
He very, very rarely feels
    As well as you and I.
His eye is dull, his head is bald,
    His neck is growing thinner.
Oh! what a lesson for us all
    To only eat at dinner!

HILAIRE BELLOC

FATTY, FATTY, BOOM-A-LATTY

Fatty, Fatty, Boom-a-latty;
  This is the way she goes!
She is so large around the waist,
  She cannot see her toes!

ANONYMOUS

FROM I Know an Old Lady

I know an old lady who swallowed a cow,
Don't ask how she swallowed a cow.
She swallowed the cow to catch the goat,
Popped open her throat and swallowed a goat.
She swallowed the goat to catch the dog,
Oh, what a hog to swallow a dog!
She swallowed the dog to catch the cat.
Think of that, she swallowed a cat!
She swallowed the cat to catch the bird.
How absurd to swallow a bird!
She swallowed the bird to catch the spider
That wiggled and jiggled and tickled inside her.
She swallowed the spider to catch the fly.
I don't know why she swallowed the fly,
Perhaps she'll die.

I know an old lady who swallowed a horse,
She died, of course!

ANONYMOUS

Who Swallowed a Fly

BETTY BOPPER

This is Little Betty Bopper.
She has popcorn in the popper.
Seven pounds of it! Please stop her.
That's more popcorn than is proper
In a popper. Someone drop her
Just a hint! Mommer! Popper!
Betty's going to come a cropper!
Look, it's starting! Get a chopper.
Chop the door down!
          . . . Well, too late.

JOHN CIARDI

40

Mary had a little lamb,
A lobster, and some prunes,
A glass of milk, a piece of pie,
And then some macaroons.

It made the busy waiters grin
To see her order so,
And when they carried Mary out,
Her face was white as snow.

ANONYMOUS

Giants' Delight

Vats of soup
On table trays
Side of shark
With mayonnaise
Haunch of ox
With piles of mice
Mounds of gristle
Served on ice
Bone of mammoth
Head of boar
Whales and serpents
By the score

Tons of cole slaw
Stacks of rabbits
(Giants have such
Piggy habits)
Then, at last,
There comes a stew
Full of buffalo
And ewe
Followed by
Some chocolate cakes
Big enough
For stomachaches

STEVEN KROLL

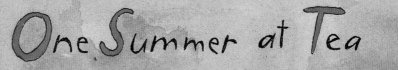

One Summer at Tea

There was a young parson named Perkins
Exceedingly fond of small gherkins
    One summer at tea
    He ate forty-three,
Which pickled his internal workings.

ANONYMOUS

I ATE TOO MUCH

I ate too much turkey,
I ate too much corn,
I ate too much pudding and pie,
I'm stuffed up with muffins
and much too much stuffin',
I'm probably going to die.
I piled up my plate
and I ate and I ate,
but I wish I had known when to stop,
for I'm so crammed with yams,
sauces, gravies, and jams
that my buttons are starting to pop.
I'm full of tomatoes
and french fried potatoes,
my stomach is swollen and sore,
but there's still some dessert,
so I guess it won't hurt
if I eat just a little bit more.

JACK PRELUTSKY

Yes, please!

Would you like some dessert?

Greedy Ned

A greedy young fellow named Ned
Ate up before going to bed—
    Six lobsters, one ham,
    Ten pickles with jam,
And when he woke up he was dead.

ANONYMOUS

My Mother Says I'm Sickening

My mother says I'm sickening,
my mother says I'm crude,
she says this when she sees me
playing Ping-Pong with my food,
she doesn't seem to like it
when I slurp my bowl of stew,
and now she's got a list of things
she says I mustn't do—

DO NOT CATAPULT THE CARROTS!
DO NOT JUGGLE GOBS OF FAT!
DO NOT DROP THE MASHED POTATOES
ON THE GERBIL OR THE CAT!
NEVER PUNCH THE PUMPKIN PUDDING!
NEVER TUNNEL THROUGH THE BREAD!
PUT NO PEAS INTO YOUR POCKET!
PLACE NO NOODLES ON YOUR HEAD!
DO NOT SQUEEZE THE STEAMED ZUCCHINI!
DO NOT MAKE THE MELON OOZE!
NEVER STUFF VANILLA YOGURT
IN YOUR LITTLE SISTER'S SHOES!
DRAW NO FACES IN THE KETCHUP!
MAKE NO LITTLE GRAVY POOLS!

I wish my mother wouldn't make
so many useless rules.

JACK PRELUTSKY

TABLE MANNERS

The Goops they lick their fingers,
 The Goops they lick their knives,
They spill their broth on the table-cloth;
 They live untidy lives.
The Goops they talk while eating,
 And loud and fast they chew,
So that is why I am glad that I
 Am not a Goop. Are you?

GELETT BURGESS

50

I eat my peas with honey;
I've done it all my life.
It makes the peas taste funny,
But it keeps them on the knife.

ANONYMOUS

THE CATSUP BOTTLE

Shake and shake
the catsup bottle.
None will come
and then a lot'll.

RICHARD ARMOUR

I dribbled catsup on my pet,
And that is why my cat's upset.

JACK PRELUTSKY

TROUBLE WITH DINNER

Why can't I dig with my spoon and make
Potato castles like on the beach?
Why aren't there sensible things to eat,
Like jam and jelly and pink-iced cake?
Why stuff like horrid cabbage and meat?
Why can't I kneel on my chair and reach?

It's quicker than saying, "Pass the sauce,"
When nobody listens and nobody will:
And such bad manners to wave or SHOUT,
And wrong to get down and fetch it, of course!
Why shouldn't I "mess my dinner about"
With Gravy River round Spinach Hill?

My knife's a dagger, my fork's a torch,
These peas are PILLS with a POISON label!
I'm Special Agent, the Prince's twin!
My mouth's a secret door in a porch,
Nobody can see what's going in—
"Just take those elbows off the table!"

"I'm sorry, Mom."—Sail through my broth . . .
"Be careful, child, you'll splash your jeans!
  There now, see what you've done! You've spilled
  Food on my nice clean tablecloth!"
"I'm sorry, Mom."—I think I'll build
  A Pharoah's Pyramid with beans.

  First make a square, and then along
  The edges lay them stone by stone . . .
"Don't use your fingers, darling—stop!"
  Why is it always me that's wrong?
  I'm sure I've often seen my Pop
  Pick up and gnaw a meaty bone.

  Yet if I tell her that, she'll say,
"Don't talk, child, with your mouth full!"—Worst,
  They do make eating such a bore,
  When it's so much more fun to play.
  There now, I've dropped some on the floor—
  I hope the puppy finds it first.

J. A. LINDON

Cooked Carrots

On way to mouth, drop in lap.
Smuggle to garbage in napkin.

Spaghetti

Wind too many strands on the fork and make sure at least two strands dangle down. Open your mouth wide and stuff in spaghetti; suck noisily to inhale the dangling strands. Clean plate, ask for seconds, and eat only half. When carrying your plate to the kitchen, hold it tilted so that the remaining spaghetti slides off and onto the floor.

54

LIKE A CHILD

FRENCH FRIES

Wave one French fry in air for emphasis while you talk. Pretend to conduct orchestra. Then place four fries in your mouth at once and chew. Turn to your sister, open your mouth, and stick out your tongue coated with potatoes. Close mouth and swallow. Smile.

Spinach

Divide into little piles. Rearrange into new piles. After five or six maneuvers, sit back and say you are full.

DELIA EPHRON

EATING AT THE RESTAURANT OF HOW CHOW NOW

Ever eaten Chinese food?
Eaten with chopsticks made of wood,
Holding one chopstick nice and tight?
The other never works just right.

Or if it does, the tight one teeters.
These wooden hinges aren't for eaters
Like you and me. We get a grip
On bamboo shoots, and off they slip!

Thin mushroom slices, peapods, rice,
Hockeypuck meat, need some device
to gather in and underslide them.
Forks are good. But Chinese hide them.

Same with knives: *they can't abide them!*

DAVID McCORD

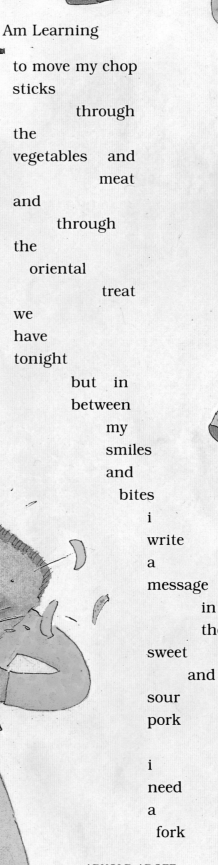

I Am Learning

to move my chop
sticks
through
the
vegetables   and
meat
and
through
the
oriental
treat
we
have
tonight
but   in
between
my
smiles
and
bites
i
write
a
message
in
the
sweet
and
sour
pork

i
need
a
fork

ARNOLD ADOFF

57

Never Take a Pig to Lunch

Never take a pig to lunch.
Don't invite him home for brunch.
Cancel chances to be fed
Till you're certain he's well-bred.

Quiz him! Can he use a spoon?
Does his sipping sing a tune?
Will he slurp and burp and snuff
Till his gurgling makes you gruff?

Would he wrap a napkin 'round
Where the dribbled gravy's found?
Tidbits nibble? Doughnuts dunk?
Spill his milk before it's drunk?

Root and snoot through soup du jour?
Can your appetite endure?
If his manners make you moan,
Better let him lunch alone.

SUSAN ALTON SCHMELTZ

from The Clean Platter

Never mind what kind of food.
Through thick and through thin
I am constantly in
The mood
For food!

OGDEN NASH

Index of Titles

Index of Poets

Copyright © 1994 by Nadine Bernard Westcott. First Orchard Paperbacks edition 1998.
All rights reserved. No part of this book may be reproduced or transmitted in any
form or by any means, electronic or mechanical, including photocopying, recording, or by any information storage or retrieval system,
without permission in writing from the Publisher. Orchard Books, 95 Madison Avenue, New York, NY 10016

The text of this book is set in 12 point Bookman. The illustrations are done with black ink line and acrylics.
Manufactured in Singapore. Printed and bound by Toppan Printing Company, Inc. Book design by Sylvia Frezzolini.

Hardcover 10 9 8 7 6 5 4 3 2   Paperback 10 9 8 7 6 5 4 3 2 1

Library of Congress Cataloging-in-Publication Data
Never take a pig to lunch : poems about the fun of eating / selected and illustrated by Nadine Bernard Westcott.
p. cm. Includes index.   Summary: A collection of poems and traditional rhymes about food and eating.
ISBN 0-531-06834-X (tr.)   ISBN 0-531-07098-0 (pbk.)
1. Food—Juvenile poetry.   2. Dinners and dining—Juvenile poetry.   3. Children's poetry, American.   4. Children's poetry, English.
[1. Food—Poetry.   2. American poetry—Collections.   3. English poetry—Collections.] I. Westcott, Nadine Bernard.
PS595.F65N48 1994 811.008'0355—dc20 93-11801

Acknowledgments

Grateful acknowledgment is made to the following for permission to use material owned by them. Every reasonable effort has been made to clear the use of the poems in this volume. If notified of any omissions, the editor and publisher will make the necessary corrections in future editions.

"I Am Learning" by Arnold Adoff from *Eats*. Text copyright © 1979 by Arnold Adoff. Reprinted by permission of Lothrop, Lee and Shepard, a division of William Morrow & Company, Inc., Publishers.

"Snow-cone" by John Agard from *I Din Do Nuttin* (Bodley Head Press, 1983). Reprinted by kind permission of John Agard c/o Caroline Sheldon Literary Agency.

"The Picnic" by Dorothy Aldis from *Hop, Skip and Jump!* Copyright 1934, © 1961 by Dorothy Aldis. Reprinted by permission of G. P. Putnam's Sons.

"The Catsup Bottle" by Richard Armour from *It All Started with Columbus*. Copyright © 1961 by Richard Armour. Reprinted by permission of McGraw-Hill, Inc.

"The Vulture" by Hilaire Belloc from *Cautionary Verses* (Alfred A. Knopf, Inc., 1941) and *Complete Verse* (Pimlico, a division of Random Century). Copyright 1931 by Hilaire Belloc. Copyright © renewed 1959 by Eleanor Jebb Belloc, Elizabeth Belloc, and Hilary Belloc. Reprinted by permission of Alfred A. Knopf, Inc., and the Peters Fraser & Dunlop Group Ltd.

"Picnics" by Marchette Chute from *Rhymes About the Country*. Copyright 1941 by The Macmillan Company. Copyright © renewed 1969 by Marchette Chute. Reprinted by permission of Elizabeth Roach.

"Betty Bopper" by John Ciardi from *Mummy Took Cooking Lessons*. Text copyright © 1990 by Judith C. Ciardi. Reprinted by permission of Houghton Mifflin Company. All rights reserved.

"A Fisherman living in Deal . . ." by Charles Connell from *Versicles and Limericks* (Red Fox). Reprinted by permission of the Random Century Group.

"Cooked Carrots," "French Fries," "Spaghetti," and "Spinach" by Delia Ephron from *How to Eat Like a Child*. Copyright © 1977, 1978 by Delia Ephron. Reprinted by permission of Viking Penguin, a division of Penguin Books USA, Inc.

Excerpt from *Slugs* by David Greenberg. Text copyright © 1983 by David Greenberg. By permission of Little, Brown and Company.

"Baloney!" and "It's Hot!" by Florence Parry Heide. Copyright © 1993 by Florence Parry Heide. "Query" by Florence Parry Heide and Roxanne Heide Pierce. Copyright © 1993 by Florence Parry Heide and Roxanne Heide Pierce. Reprinted by permission of Curtis Brown, Ltd.

"What You Don't Know About Food" by Florence Parry Heide from *Grim and Ghastly Goings-On*. Text copyright © 1992 by Florence Parry Heide. Reprinted by permission of Lothrop, Lee and Shepard Books, a division of William Morrow & Company, Inc., Publishers.

"School Lunch" by Mary Ann Hoberman. Copyright © 1993 by Mary Ann Hoberman. "Yellow Butter" by Mary Ann Hoberman from *Yellow Butter, Purple Jelly, Red Jam, Black Bread*. Copyright © 1981 by Mary Ann Hoberman. Reprinted by permission of Gina Maccoby Literary Agency.

"Oodles of Noodles" by Lucia and James L. Hymes, Jr., from *Oodles of Noodles*. Copyright © 1964 by Addison-Wesley Publishing Company, Inc. Reprinted with permission of the publisher.

"Lasagna" (one stanza of "Italian Noodles") by X. J. Kennedy from *Ghastlies, Goops & Pincushions*. Copyright © 1979, 1989 by X. J. Kennedy. Reprinted with permission of Margaret K. McElderry Books, an imprint of Macmillan Publishing Company.

"Giants' Delight" by Steven Kroll from *Giant Poems*. Copyright © 1978 by Holiday House, Inc. Reprinted by permission of Writers House, Inc.

"Trouble with Dinner" by J. A. Lindon. Reprinted by permission of Frank R. Lindon.

"O Sliver of Liver" by Myra Cohn Livingston from *O Sliver of Liver and Other Poems*. Copyright © 1979 by Myra Cohn Livingston. Reprinted by permission of Marian Reiner for the author.

"Eating at the Restaurant of How Chow Now" by David McCord from *For Me to Say*. Copyright © 1970 by David McCord. By permission of Little, Brown and Company.

"How Do You Make a Pizza Grow?" and "I Want My Breakfast the Giant Said" by Eve Merriam from *Blackberry Ink*. Copyright © 1985 by Eve Merriam. "Peculiar" by Eve Merriam from *Jamboree: Rhymes for All Times*. Copyright © 1962, 1964, 1966, 1973, 1984 by Eve Merriam. Reprinted by permission of Marian Reiner.

"Eels" by Spike Milligan from *A Book of Bits or a Bit of a Book*. Reprinted by permission of Norma Farnes.

"Said a Long Crococile" by Lilian Moore from *See My Lovely Poison Ivy*. Copyright © 1975 by Lilian Moore. Reprinted by permission of Marian Reiner for the author.

Excerpt from "The Clean Platter" by Ogden Nash from *Custard and Company*. Copyright 1935 by Ogden Nash. "Celery," "The Eel," and "The Parsnip" by Ogden Nash from *Verses from 1929 On*. Copyright 1941, 1942 by Ogden Nash. "Experiment Degustatory" by Ogden Nash from *There's Always Another Windmill*. Copyright © 1966 by Ogden Nash. "Celery" and "Experiment Degustatory" first appeared in *The Saturday Evening Post*. "The Eel" first appeared in *The New Yorker*. By permission of Little, Brown and Company.

"Fudge" and "Spaghetti! Spaghetti!" by Jack Prelutsky from *Rainy Rainy Saturday*. Text copyright © 1980 by Jack Prelutsky. "I Ate Too Much" by Jack Prelutsky from *It's Thanksgiving*. Text copyright © 1982 by Jack Prelutsky. "My Mother Says I'm Sickening" by Jack Prelutsky from *The New Kid on the Block*. Text copyright © 1984 by Jack Prelutsky. By permission of Greenwillow Books, a division of William Morrow & Company, Inc., Publishers.

"I dribbled catsup . . ." by Jack Prelutsky from *The Poems of A. Nonny Mouse* selected by Jack Prelutsky. Copyright © 1989 by Jack Prelutsky. Reprinted by permission of Alfred A. Knopf, Inc.

"Never Take a Pig to Lunch" by Susan Alton Schmeltz. Copyright by Susan M. Schmeltz. Originally published in *Cricket*, Vol. 4, No. 5, January 1977. Reprinted by permission of the author.

"Tomatoes, lettuce . . ." appeared in *And the Green Grass Grew All Around: Folk Poetry from Everyone* by Alvin Schwartz. Text © 1992 by Alvin Schwartz. HarperCollins Publishers.

"Eating with an Alligator Isn't Quite the Thing!" by Angela Sidey. Reprinted by permission of the author.

"Arbuckle Jones" by Peter Wesley-Smith from *The Ombley-Gombley*. Reprinted by permission of Angus & Robertson Publishers.

"Peanut Butter and Jelly" by Nadine Bernard Westcott from *Peanut Butter and Jelly: A Play Rhyme*. Copyright © 1987 by Nadine Bernard Westcott. Reprinted by permission of Dutton Children's Books, a division of Penguin Books USA, Inc.

"Successful Pancakes," by Charles Wilkins from *Do Whales Jump at Night?* edited by Florence McNeil. Douglas & McIntyre, 1990. "A (Pretty) Good Recipe for Pie" by Charles Wilkins from *Old Mrs. Schmatterbung and Other Friends*. McClelland & Stewart, 1990. Reprinted by permission of the author.

All titles not listed above are in the public domain and are reprinted in various works.